The Leadership Principle

Kenneth W. Gilmore, Sr.

Copyright © 2002 by Kenneth W. Gilmore Sr.

The Leadership Principle

by Kenneth W. Gilmore Sr.

Printed in the United States of America

ISBN 09729275-3-0

All rights reserved. No part of this publication may be reproduced or transmitted in any form or by any means without written permission of the publisher.

Unless otherwise quoted, all Scripture quotations are from the Holy Bible, New King James Version. Copyright © 1982 Thomas Nelson, Inc.

Scripture quotations marked NASB are taken from the NEW AMERICAN STANDARD BIBLE?®, Copyright © 1960, 1962, 1963, 1971, 1972, 1973, 1975, 1977, 1995 by The Lockman Foundation. Used by permission.

Published by Kenneth W. Gilmore, Sr. Ministries

Dedication

This book is dedicated to Buford Shields (deceased), who is my father in the gospel. He started me in the ministry and the first expository preacher that I was exposed to.

To Dr. Andrew J. Hairston who taught and molded biblical leadership for me.

And also to Dr. Carl Spain (deceased), my professor of Bible and ministry at Abilene Christian University, Abliene Texas. He taught me the principles of biblical leadership.

Table Of Contents

INTRODUCTION

The purpose of this book is to give voice—openly and without censorship and polarization—what many of our people already think—that there must be change. The current leadership in our churches, as it reflects in terms of progressiveness, is dismal at best. Churches that were one-time beacons across our brotherhood are currently experiencing rapid decline from the West Coast to the East Coast, North to Middle America.

This is hemorrhaging in our national psyche as a brotherhood. A new vision for the church is desperately needed. This calls for more than just cosmetic changes in the basic infrastructure of our churches. If our fellowship refuses to look at the underpinning of our structures, we fail to see what really holds us together.

For the last five years, I have coordinated leadership and church growth conferences across the United States. In 1990, I began to understand why some churches grow and some churches don't grow. I thought, maybe it is because some churches are more biblical, or they love God more than others, or they are more godly.

Truly, each of these reasons are important, but they have little to do with the growth and expansion of your church. In 1994, I decided to further my research and inquiry while working on a doctorate in Leadership at Pepperdine University. Coupled with my undergraduate and master's degrees in Bible and Religion, I wanted to evaluate and assess Leadership Theory and Organizational Development in the context of theology.

I was amazed at the similarity that runs through secular organizations as they sought to make their companies competitive in the global economy. The ingredient that I found in my research was the nature and character of why churches grow and some do not—it was the essential ingredient of leadership.

In recent years in African-American Churches of Christ, debate has arisen over the ordination of elders for church government in the local church. There are excellent books on the elders and their role in the local church. I have come to realize that simply ordaining elders in a local church may even complicate the leadership problem in the local church. Luis Lugo has done an excellent job in defining the role of the evangelist in the local church. In my judgment, these two offices are biblical and they are needed, yet they still do not resolve the lack of leadership in the local church—at least those who assume these biblical roles are not leaders.

We all know good leaders when we see them, and if you ask each of us to define leadership, we would all come up with different definitions because the word "leadership" is such a nebulous term to define. In this book, I have not set out to exhaustively or comprehensively deal with the subject of leadership.

I would invite the reader to look at the seminal work of Ralph Stodgill's *Handbook on Leadership*, which is the definitive, most comprehensive and exhaustive book on the subject of leadership in any circle—academic, professional, religious. Anything that has been written on the subject of leadership from Machiavelli up to the contemporary works are indexed in Stodgill's handbook. I would suggest that you purchase it. The cost is approximately $100, but it will be worth the investment.

In the first section of this book, I talk about the Crisis of Leadership. Theories of Leadership, Qualities of Leadership, and Skills of Leadership. Some may ask, why a book on church leadership? The church that we have known for the past fifty years no longer exists. A different generation has arrived; the issues of our day are different. To continue to use the same old vehicle, concepts, arguments, or polemics that have brought us where we are today will continue to bring only decline and death.

Our churches are dying. Our members are leaving our ranks to find fertile soils to replant themselves for future growth. They attend Caucasian or other denominational congregations to find leadership that is not controlled by leaders who are autocratic in their leadership style. Leaders continue to preach a rigid, narrow theology to people Sunday after Sunday. Members come to be healed but leave our assemblies with heads and hearts still wounded and their hands empty. The following issues are critical to the growth of our churches and our fellowship:

- The time has come when African-American Churches of Christ need overhauling in our worship, educational system, music, and outreach.

- There are leaders among our ranks who have quietly left our national forums because they see them only as competitive platforms for preachers to stroke their own egos and compete for gospel meetings. They do not see the critical issues that face us as a people and our fellowship. They could provide a forum to discuss meaningful ways to fund and support vital projects that could help us to critically evaluate and strengthen the Restoration Movement among African Americans.
- A national clearing-house needs to be established for the publication of books, church material, and educational curriculum. We simply have no organizational structure as a national body. This clearing-house does not have to violate the local leadership of a congregation.
- At last count, based on statistics compiled by Dr. Mac Lynn of David Lipscomb University, stated that about

1,200 African-American Churches of Christ with a total membership nationwide of 98,732 are not enough to populate a city like Tyler, Texas. States such as Texas, Tennessee, Florida, California, Alabama, and Georgia have memberships, with each exceeding 2,000. The question to be raised is why has the growth declined? When Keeble, Bowser, Hogan, Kennedy, Stewart, Winston and others baptized thousands in their generation, they were less equipped than leaders today and yet they made incredible inroads in their time.

- A new vision challenges us to critically look at this issue of autonomy, as it relates to each church being unique in its own indigenous ministry context. The community (people, needs, resources) determines what vision and ministry are best suitable for that church. This challenges us to look seriously at re-evaluating the franchise concept that many of our churches have adopted.

The purpose of the franchise concept like McDonald's is that you can find the same Big Mac and golden fries everywhere you go. Our purpose is to identify and preserve the New Testament church. Our goal is to make sure that every church you visit in this nation or internationally serves up the same prototype.

The franchise concept has paralyzed our worship through artificiality and ritualism. Our assemblies have no vitality or creativity. Furthermore, each local congregation is autonomous to govern its own affairs, but when one church breaks rank with the parade, we ostracize, alienate it, and withdraw fellowship, which is inconsistent with the use of autonomy.

There is no New Testament example of churches ever withdrawing from another congregation. We come to the New Testament preconditioned by our own experiences and what we have been taught to see, not understanding that the church in the New Testament was still very much in its embryonic state. It was still developing and hammering out positions on certain issues as it confronted them in their indigenous setting, which may be a way for us to solve some of our problems.

This can be clearly seen in those letters ascribed to Paul's authorship.

There were core issues that many early Christians were not clear on as they related to the virgin birth, clearly seen in John's writings. The resurrection and the Lord's Supper as evident in the Corinthian correspondence. The second coming of Jesus in I and II Thessalonians. The issues discussed concerning marriage, divorce, and remarriage in the Gospels and Paul's teaching. Race relations between Jew and Gentiles in Romans, Galatians, and Acts. It is quite evident that the early Christian movement was experiencing tension, ambiguity, and uncertainty, and these Christians were very much tolerant of each other's views before they built barriers.

A new vision challenges us to look at the sacred cows of our fellowship. A sacred cow is any tradition, custom, practice, culture, or a way of thinking that has become the norm or the principle of operation. It is a philosophy of reasoning, an interpretation to maintain the status quo.

Biblical Interpretation

Churches of Christ have been described as people of the book. Our motto emerged out of the Restoration Movement, "Speak where the Bible speaks, and be silent where the Bible is silent." This statement is a paraphrase of I Peter 4:11: "If any man speaks, let him speak as the oracles of God." With the rise of the historical critical method of interpretation coming out of Germany in the early 1800s in addition to early Lockeian, the stage was set to critique the Bible as a literary piece and to search for the sources of the original autographs. The science of textual criticism was born. The emphasis was to establish the text. Buzz words like "Exegesis—what does the text say, to Hermeneutics—what does it mean" has become a part of our religious vocabulary in our churches.

We have leaders who give us the distinct impression that they are scholars spouting their Greek words. When you ask these leaders: "What case is this noun in? Is it objective or subjective genitive? Is this verb in the present tense or in the imperative mode? Is it in the perfect tense or pluperfect? A mute expression begins to appear across their faces. We use Greek lexicons, such as Thayer's Lexicon, which, when first published, had become obsolete with the discovery of the papyrus manuscripts (see Adolf Diessman's *Light from the Ancient East*).

The abuse of the use of the Greek is the very warning that James Barr mentioned in his seminal work, *The Semantics of Biblical Languages*. Defining words simply on the origin and usage of a word in isolation from the context does a grave injustice to good exegesis. Barr further argues that the New Testament writers were not oriented to Greek culture, but definitely Hebraic in thought patterns. To simply quote this is a misrepresentation and carelessness of the use of Greek in our churches and pulpits.

There is currently a great deal of interest concerning the "New Hermeneutics" in our congregations. The concern for many older church members is whether the younger generation is leaving the old paths and removing the ancient landmarks. Both at the 1994 and 2002 Southwestern Christian College Lectureship, a forum was held to discuss a number of key platform issues that traditionally the Churches of Christ have held onto so tenaciously—instrumental music, Christians only, baptism, and so forth—with the defenders of the faith well on display to roll back the tide of liberalism, as they defined it. The forum raised the issue that our way of interpreting the Bible is the only way to interpret the Bible. The questions must be asked: Who determines what form of interpretation is correct? What were the other forms of interpretation that were not selected? When did this occur? How much does culture impact interpretation? Is not the current standard of interpretation Euro centric?

The Role of Women in the Church

This critical issue will rip our fellowship apart if leadership is not given in this area and address the frustrations of many educated, gifted, spiritual women who make up 75 to 85 percent of our churches. Our interpretation of text, such as I Corinthians 14:34 and I Timothy 2, supports our religious dogmatism to control and manipulate women and keep them under subjection. In our pursuit to be biblically sound, we ignore other related passages of powerful and purposeful role of women in biblical history. Deborah, who as a judge, made tough decisions concerning legal matters as they confronted the people of God; Esther, Queen of Persia, sought to save a nation. Elizabeth gave birth to John the Baptist, the forerunner of the Lord. Mary was the mother of the Savior. The husband and wife team of Aquinas and Priscilla; Lydia's conversion which opened the door to European evangelism.

We fail in our attempt to exegete passages such as I Corinthians, Chapters 11 and 14, in the context of prophetic utterances in public worship of the church. We fail to clearly understand the magnitude of Galatians 3:28 that says gender, race, and class have no place in the Kingdom of God. Leaders in Churches of Christ believe that leadership is defined and restricted to the genitalia of the male anatomy. Our refusal to see the cultural impact of Jewish, Greek, and Roman cultures in the Scriptures and its impact on church policy have led to faulty exegesis. Our ministry positions are being exclusively controlled on gender alone. Many of these women are spiritually and intellectually more competent to lead churches than many of our men. We need to examine I Corinthians 11 and 14; I Timothy 2;

Genesis 3; Romans 16:1; Galatians 3:26-27 and the doctrine of Usurpation of Authority.

The Plan of Salvation

Many feel that you have not preached unless you mentioned the five steps—hear, believe, repent, confess, and be baptized—which has no precedent anywhere in the New Testament. It is our deductive and rationalistic thinking engendered by the Age of Enlightenment. We do not want to give historical credence that it started with John Walter Scott to teach children so they could encourage their parents to attend his camp meeting revival. We must simply preach about Christ. We never see the Apostles ever advocating the organism to the exclusion of the head, but Christ who adds them to His Body, study the sermons in Luke in Acts.

Methods of Evangelism

Among African-American Churches of Christ, the methods of evangelism are door knocking, the Jules Miller film strips, handing out Bible tracks, gospel meetings, and crusades. Whether they are citywide or nationwide does not increase our membership for the amount of money expended. If careful follow-up and tracking procedures were instigated on the people who have come to Christ through these vehicles, the data would be surprising about the retention rates. Yet many of us know this and we continue to repeat the same old failures. We should explore other methods of evangelism, such as small groups—cell groups—and friendship evangelism. Many who come to Christ come as the result of a friend who first introduced them to Christ. Why not invest our money wisely in training our people in "lifestyle evangelism." Real ministry involves a real investment of time. We who are stewards of God's resources must give an account of how we used God's money.

Leadership Development

"Everything rises and falls on leadership." Many leaders in our churches are intensely debating the issues of elders and who is in charge—the elders or the preacher. In my judgment, these issues fail to deal honestly with the crisis of leadership in African-American Churches of Christ. Some believe once we ordain elders that they will serve as a panacea for all the ills of our fellowship. We choose to ignore Paul's admonition that many of the problems the church would face would come from the inner circle of the elders. The real issue is vision, leadership, and people skills. Leaders are always challenged to deal with our own frail egos, as Paul admonishes his two prodigies, Timothy and Titus, in the pastoral letters. Why is it that a preacher who has served the church for thirty years has not trained any leaders to succeed him once he is gone? Why is it that leadership development is non-existent in our congregation?

Chapter One
Leadership

There are three purposes for this chapter. I want to look at the systemic factors that have contributed to the decline and apathy among contemporary African-American Churches of Christ, to call the church to a new vision that is rooted in the best of our tradition and heritage, and to propose solutions to the leadership crisis in African-American Churches of Christ.

The Crisis of Leadership

Among contemporary African-American Churches of Christ is a thirst and grasp for power, not unlike that which exists in society, and it has infiltrated and contaminated our fellowship at an alarming rate. Membership is in decline. Apathy exists among the ranks. Leaders who are promiscuous are unrestrained with prudence, and they run the landscape of our brotherhood. Those who are reputed to be pillars of the church refuse to rescind membership within the fraternity of preachers, while their activities bring disgrace to the ministry and bring the priesthood under a cloud of shame. No criteria or standard exists for entrance into the ministry. Anyone without ordination, confirmation, or training can become a leader among us. This is indicative of the present crisis we face as a national body.

Leaders run the church as if the church is the German Gestapo. Members' lives are toyed with as though they are pawns in a chess game. Dictatorship and manipulation reign. Pseudo positions of power and influence are fought over. Polarization of splits are created, walls are built, and the church is left to retreat into its stained-glass foxholes. We wave the flag of truce but have discovered that the real enemy is us. Leaders need to come together in a national summit and begin the process to address the central issues that face us as a national body. From east to west, north to south, congregations are hemorrhaging, dying for lack of attention to a compelling vision, a dynamic leadership, relevant ministries, and a celebratory worship experience.

The African-American community is disintegrating before our very eyes, yet the church seems to be helpless or has misdirected priorities. Leaders continue to invest millions of God's money into programs that are inadequate to provide real ministry to our people. Dr. Kenneth Greene describes this paralysis that has gripped our fellowship by labeling it "insiderism." Insiderism is the paralyzing of thought, when leaders are interested only in serving the institution instead of people. Programs are irrelevant and personnel are out of touch with the needs of the community. We come to our comfortable buildings and wonder why our churches are not effective in their outreach. Worship has become poisoned with ritualism and boredom.

The reality of God has been replaced by artificiality and staleness. Insiderism has also caused us to debate about issues that have no real value or meaning as they relate to everyday living. Many of our members pay lip service, but their behavior contradicts these same issues. We have caused our people to be intellectually and theologically dishonest.

Paul, writing to the Church at Corinth,

clearly warned that party rivalry in the church is not conducive to growth and maturation. We have not learned to resolve our conflicts before we let them escalate into an acute crisis. The church needs men and women who are willing to sacrifice their own agendas for the success and promulgation of the gospel. The church is not a democracy and neither is it a place where tyranny reigns, but the church is where men and women coexist in mutual love and concern—a theocracy.

The church is a model—the place where God has experimented as to how the rest of the world should be. Francis Schaeffer described a society where the church had lost its purpose and direction as the world looks for guidance and moral courage. The questions that he leaves the reader to ponder are: What happens to our society when we, as the people of God, have lost our heritage and have forgotten our legacy? What shall become of us? Will we exist or perish? Will we die and see the moment of greatness flicker? The church has languished too long in the corners, basements, and alleys of the world. Let her come out into the sunshine, rise up, and stake out her claim upon the soul of the world. If she abandons her birthright, she must fasten the shutter and lower the anchor of her ships for the clouds are full of rain and the storms fast approaching. Will she sink or will she swim?

The Mission

What is destroying the church is not the outward groping of those within or the inward groping of those without, but the professionals who control it and who have removed the bells from its steeples. In Europe and early Colonial America, churches were constructed with bells in the steeples to announce significant moments that affected the life of the community—fire, death, birth, and time. They served as a wake-up call, a rallying cry to the community. Churches were the center of community life, the anchor, a place of stability, holding up a transcendent vision of the meaning of life.

Our contemporary fellowship must ask itself one question: Who removed the bells from the steeples? African Americans are looking to the church and her leaders to ring out a clear and sure message of faith and hope. They are hungering for a compelling message and commitment to an essential vision for our people.

Leadership, both local and national, must re-examine the church's purpose for existence. Historically, Churches of Christ have focused entirely on eradicating denominationalism. We have never truly focused theologically on the mission of the church. I contend that the mission of the church is not to debate and teach against denominationalism, but the ultimate vision and mission—the transformation of human life. Church leaders must assess and evaluate their congregations and church ministries in the context of whether lives are being changed in the context of mission. Do not let the church follow the example of Rip Van Winkle who slept for twenty years and realized that the world in which he lived had radically changed.

The Church as a System

We need to constantly look at the dynamics of congregational life in our churches because churches, by definition, are social systems in which there are norms, values, and shared beliefs. The problem with our existing leadership training is that young leaders leave seminary to become leaders in congregations, and they do not recognize the culture in those churches. When conflict emerges in those congregations, these leaders are ill-equipped to diagnose problems in the congregational system.

Failure in resolving conflict is to misunderstand the dynamics of congregational life. Many church leaders are trained to view the church only as a theological entity rather than to assess our congregations through organizational theory, group processes, and sociology. Problems that are not easily diagnosed in theological or psychological categories can be observed through basic social principles that operate in all human organizations, including congregations. When leaders recognize the church as a system, we then can see the social indicators that interface with our congregations and that permit us to be generative in our mission rather than adaptive.

Generative Learning Versus Adaptive Learning

Peter Senge, in his book, *The Fifth Discipline*, speaks of organizations that are generative rather than adaptive. These organizations will survive and succeed because they constantly scan the social and political environment of their surroundings. Organizations are affected by other systems within the environment.

The church must become a learning organization where leaders, staff, and members continually expand the capacity to create the results they truly desire for the church—where new and creative ideas of thinking are nurtured, when collective aspirations are set free, and where the church continues to learn together. Leaders must see that the church is a social institution, a system where all elements (worship, outreach, music, program development, and education) operate as an interdependent entity.

When leaders recognize the church as a social system, they can then understand the importance of generative learning. Generative learning affords leaders the capability to fully socialize people into the life of the church. This process is achieved through ideological orientation. Ideological orientation is the system of thought by which members make sense of the church. The ideology functions to give members cognitive maps by which they make their way into the church system, and provides justification for the way the church treats people and relates to society.

The church's body of ideas is an ideological system that shapes the process of the church. Leaders must provide members cognitive maps by which they can make their way in the world, as well as the church. The business of the church is to preach—to set forth a road map for life. Most organizations are not forced to articulate their ideology as often as the church does. But every organization is judged at some level and whether or not it practices what it preaches. Generative learning forces leaders to look at the factors that have contributed to their decline and lack of growth. Leaders just look at their behavioral patterns that may keep us from being pro-active as a church and visionary in our thinking.

Adaptive Learning

Senge defines adaptive learning as survival learning. When leaders are in the adaptive mode, they react to crisis rather than being preventive and creative about issues that may be a possible threat to our survival. Adaptive learning forces us to hold on to our sacred cows; sacred cows are traditions, customs, practices, ways of thinking, a culture that has become the norm or the principle of operation. It is a philosophy of reasoning, an interpretation to maintain the status quo. It is homeostasis or ossification, the inability to grow and expand our thinking (for example, biblical interpretation, the role of women, the King James version, plan of salvation, church autonomy, music).

Adaptive learning allows the church the unfortunate pleasure of thinking nostalgic about victories of the past. When nostalgia sets in, it is a signal toward the trend of lack of trust, unstable relationships, and erosion of commitment to present programs and ministries. Nostalgia is the feeling of being caught betwixt and between. The future threatens and the past seems familiar and attractive. The church loses faithful and vibrant members who leave our assemblies to find fresh, fertile soil to replant themselves to grow. It leaves the heart palpitating and wrenching hands of what to do next.

What Is to Be Done?

How do we capture a new spirit and vision to meet the challenges of a post-modern culture of gender tensions, inner-city realism, denominational decline, preaching preference, and cultural sensitivity in which the church finds itself becoming more irrelevant to the needs of the African-American community? Cornell West, in his book, *Race Matters*, quoting from Abraham Lincoln, stated that only a visionary leadership can motivate the better angels of our nature. . . . Only that kind of leadership deserves cultivation and support. . . . It will take leaders to understand human nature and to believe that our churches and communities can change for good.

It will take new leaders who can look beyond the present elites and voices in leadership who recycle the older rhetoric of the past. It will take new leaders who can situate themselves within the historical narrative of religious traditions and grapple with the complex dynamics or our peoplehood.

These new leaders will be men and women who understand the dynamics of leadership and who see the pervasive erosion of our cities. Let me propose what I believe is the appropriate leadership for the crisis we are currently experiencing. African-American Churches of Christ are in need of a leadership that is based upon the premise of man's capacity for human goodness. This kind of leadership must be based upon influence, that is, both transactional and transformational.

Leadership Is Influence

Joseph Rost in his book, *Leadership*, defined leadership as a relationship among leaders and followers who intend real changes that reflect their mutual purposes. Leadership is a relationship that exists between leaders and followers. This relationship must be based upon character and credibility. It is not a relationship that is built upon Machiavellian principles of coercion and manipulation. Leadership, as influence, describes the kind of behavior that leaders must have toward their followers that they are willing to empower their people. When leaders function out of the matrix that people are to be valued and appreciated, it creates a dialogue and consensus as to what needs to be accomplished. Jesus taught that noncoercive leadership, the servant model, was the leadership style to be preferred for his people.

Leadership, as influence, widens the circle of leadership to others because there are different levels of relationship within every organization. For church leaders this is a vital leadership principle. As John Maxwell in his book *Developing the Leader Within You* states, the key to effective leadership is influencing those who influence others. Influencers are in every congregation, and they determine much of what happens in meetings. Leaders have to know who the influencers are, whose opinions matter most, and whose views others listen to and respect. When these are ignored or overlooked, they can lead the opposition and make their lives miserable.

If our churches and communities will change, it will be because leaders believe in their potential for rebirth. This process begins with our basic assumptions about human nature. How we cultivate and nurture the human spirit will determine whether we will succeed or fail.

Leadership Is Transactional

Leadership is transactional. It is the process where one takes the initiative in making contact with others for the purpose of an exchange of valued things. Leadership and followership are mutual activities of influence and counter-influence. Leaders and followers both give and receive benefits. It involves a trading of benefits. What is it that leaders receive from the followers? And what is it that followers receive from their leaders? The benefits that leaders receive from followers is the exercise of power by mobilizing competing and conflicting interests through the satisfaction of the motive bases of their followers. Robert Burns in his book, *Transformational Leadership*, further defines leadership as inducing followers to act for certain goals that represent the values and motivations—the wants and needs, the aspirations and expectations—of both leaders and followers. This mutual exchange could be economic, political, or psychological in nature.

Leadership Is Transformational

Burns further contends that the kind of leadership that does not capriciously wield power but instead acts on the behalf of followers if transformational. Transformational leadership is different from transactional in that one enters into a mutual relationship in exchange for goods or services. Transformational leadership occurs as a result of this engagement that both leader and followers raise one another to higher levels of motivation and morality. This relationship becomes a moral leadership, for example, as Martin Luther, King, Jr., Malcolm X, Gandhi, and Jesus of Nazareth raised the level of human conduct and ethical aspirations among their followers.

This kind of leadership is transcending. It challenges church leaders to appeal to the best of the human spirit and to transform our churches and communities into havens of brotherhood and love. Church leaders need to follow the example of the Reverend Johnny Youngblood who saw his church surrounded by a landscape of tenement and housing projects, of vacant lots where factories once stood, and locked and barred bungalows where decent people still tried to live. The forces of poverty, racism, and industrial decline contributed to the high crime. He built a church that transformed the community by developing strategic alliances with business, schools, city government, and law enforcement. Youngblood serves as a testament of transformational leadership at its zenith. Will we rise to the level of transformational leadership?

The Social Impact upon African-American Churches of Christ

In this chapter, I will first explore the social impact of management theory and technology upon congregational development among African-American Churches of Christ. I will look at traditional training and development for church leaders. I will also describe the role of the minister as church manager. There have been several models of what ministers are supposed to be—Christian educators, counselors, community organizers, consultants, and pastoral managers. But underneath it all, ministers are struggling to understand their role. While many seminary students receive training in psychology in preparation for pastoral counseling, few learn about principles of management and leadership in preparation for congregational leadership.

In American society, there is general agreement that the most important institution for African Americans is the black church. With new trends and technology ever on the horizon, it is imperative that African-American Churches of Christ are on the cutting edge of management and leadership. The church needs to produce leaders and staff with opportunities to acquire and sharpen their management skills and to maximize the utilization of human and financial resources. This is paramount to the success of many African-American Churches of Christ. To critically assess specific needs, church leaders must direct their attention to administrative operations, financial planning, leadership development, and human resources. These are vital issues to which church leaders must attend.

The emergence of Churches of Christ among African Americans had its early origin in the 19th century under such leaders as G.P. Bowser and Marshall Keeble. The current membership of this national body is 160,570 (Lynn). There are five factors that have contributed to the growth and stabilization of Churches of Christ among African Americans: 1) the role of G.P. Bowser and Marshall Keeble; 2) the establishment of Southwestern

Christian College, a four-year college that educates ministerial leaders for African-American Churches of Christ; 3) the establishment of the annual national lectureship; 4) the Civil Rights Movement; and 5) the role of the black preachers. These historical factors have influenced the psyche of this national movement to the extent that its churches are organized around the issue of evangelism. Very little attention to institutional management and leadership have been given to shape its ultimate mission and transforming society.

African-American Churches of Christ have given little attention to other expressions of faith, structure, decision-making, political processes, human relations, policy and procedures that govern membership conduct. When problems emerge, church leaders are not equipped to recognize the organization factors that produce conflict. When members with other perspectives observed mismanagement of church resources, they are often labeled as misinformed, troublesome, or unspiritual.

Many church leaders enter the ministry expecting to focus on preaching, prayer, and spiritual guidance. However, they soon discover that the realities of church life require working with structures and administering both to and through people. The mechanism utilized for equipping and organizing the efforts of people in the church is an integral and important function of management. This is often the difference that arises between an effective and frustrated ministry.

In today's vast and complex society, church leaders are being called to even greater challenges of leading the church into the 21st century. In a conference several years ago, 300 church leaders were invited to attend a summit in Orlando, Florida, under the leadership of Bob Buford and Fred Smith. The summit was designed to focus on the rapid and complex changes occurring in society as the church moved into the 21st century. The focus of the summit was on developing and enhancing entrepreneurial leadership and management skills that have been successful in large corporations that could be adapted within a church culture. The summit included workshops that focused on human development, handling transitions in culture, organizational structures, and the personal and professional lives of church leaders. The motivating philosophy behind this conference was to discover new ways of doing ministry in a post-modern world.

Leadership in the church requires competent administration that is sensitive to the needs of its members as it seeks to build an effective ministry. The minister needs to be familiar with all aspects of church life.

Chapter Two

Technology and Ministry

As churches continue to grow and move into the 21st century, church leaders will rely heavily on computer hardware and software to help ensure greater management of the church's financial and human resources. To incorporate technology in the church will require a substantial investment in hardware, software, and network systems. By investing in technology, it affords church leaders optimal productivity and efficiency. Church leaders will come to realize that in many ways their churches are midsize companies. With revenue in African-American churches at approximately $1 billion annually, it is imperative that ministers be effective managers of their church's resources.

There is currently on the market a variety of software packages, for example, Integrated Church Management Systems to handle record-keeping, which can do large mail-outs, quarterly and year-end reports. Roll Call allows the church to track individual members, record attendance for services, and track donations that can easily facilitate the church's ministry.

The Church as a Unique Organization

The church is unique from all other organizations. Its uniqueness is rooted in its mission to be a redemptive community of faith to build up the life of its members and to engage in a task in which its own life is to be poured out for the good of others. The church operates on the assumption that it is doing something that is of eternal value. The church by its very nature, the worshiping community, is unique and different. It is called into existence to advance a mission by the proclamation of its message which is the transformation of human life. Church leaders must be very careful in the utilization of management principles to keep a clear demarcation between the church's mission and the church's day-to-day operation.

What Is the Bottom Line?

Profit-making corporations have one criteria for self-evaluation that is specific, widely agreed upon, relatively easy to measure, and simple to understand. How much money are we making? Are profits up or down? How does this quarter compare with the same quarter a year ago? But how is the church to measure what is happening to the spiritual formation of its members? Is there an increase in baptisms? Are stewardship receipts up or down from last year? How strong is the evangelistic ministry? Are members more devout than they were last year? Is the membership increasing or decreasing? These are the questions that church leaders find difficult to assess and answer by one single yardstick, and many of these criteria are subjective and difficult to measure.

Profit-making businesses are guided by the doctrine of economic rationality. A cost-benefit analysis is the appropriate managerial procedure. By contrast, the church has a different basis for decision-making. Traditions, rituals, ceremonials, customs, schedules, and practices do not make economic sense but are very important in advancing the cause of

Christ. Business leaders would assess the profitability of a program or product, and, depending upon its success or failure, would determine whether a product or department will be down-sized. Church leaders recognize that some ministry programs may not add any financial benefit or increase to members, but they do contribute to the emotional and psychological well-being of members.

Personnel

Business leaders expect employees to produce and perform. Management operates under the assumption that it has two basic tools for motivating workers—the carrot and the stick. These have been expressed through economic rewards, promotions, suspensions, and dismissals. In contrast, churches motivate staff and members by the weight of tradition, peer group pressure, admonitions. These motivations are based on a commitment to the cause, seniority, tenure, loyalty to the organization, internalized norms, and hope for a sudden change in the person's attitudes and behavior.

The church, as an organization, as well as

other institutions, is undergoing rapid change. Society has become increasingly anti-institutional, anti-authority. The church must develop new structures of management that facilitate the church's ministry in a highly volatile and complex world. The creation of new management structures is vital and no church can exist without structure. Church leaders must develop structures of management that express the values and commitments of their congregations. Currently, apathy exists among the ranks of the membership. Leadership and management structures are autocratic and intrusive into people's lives. When management structures do not enable members to achieve personal goals that are not important to them, apathy, discontent, and conflict will abort the church's mission to which it is called to give its life.

Traditional Roles of Ministers

Many seminaries have prepared church leaders to be excellent preachers and theologians, but have done a dismal job at best to prepare ministers to serve congregations effectively as church managers. In a survey conducted by George Barna, founder and president of the Barna Research Group Ltd., the results tabulated in his book, *Today's Pastors*, strike an alarming bell that traditional theological education is out of step in training ministerial candidates for the ministry. The emphasis in seminary training is one's ability to compete by academic standards in an academic environment. Performance is measured by writing papers, passing exams, participating in classroom procedure, and class attendance. The course work required of students in the Master of Divinity Program says a lot about what seminaries seek to achieve. The required courses often relate to theology. It would be very difficult to find a course in church administration or church leadership. When a leader enters the local church, culture shock sets in because the new church leader is not equipped to manage a church. Leaders soon discover that the courses they took in systematic theology and parsing of Greek and Hebrew verbs have very little to do with conducting a business meeting, setting budgets, developing a strategic plan, building morale—the essential skills to effectively manage a church.

Traditionally, the African-American church

had its roots in slavery in antebellum South. The black church became a prophetic voice crying in the wilderness, speaking against slavery, segregation, and Jim Crow. It has been the only institution where African Americans were not under the control of white Americans. The black preacher and the pulpit followed the long history of the 8th century Hebrew prophets of the Old Testament who cried out against social and political injustice. Men such as Frederick Douglass, Nat Turner, Adam Clayton Powell, Jr., and Dr. Martin Luther King, Jr., are just a few examples of the prophetic tradition. So the black church and the black preacher have always followed the tradition of critiquing society at large.

In addition to being social critics, black preachers have maintained a balance between the prophetic and the priestly ministry. The priestly ministry in reality is making the church a place for the social outcast, the downtrodden, the dispossessed, and the powerless. If the church did not provide a haven from an insane world, it would be remiss in its pastoral and priestly function. The black preacher and the pulpit rallied a nation of 30 million African Americans to rise to their feet and march. But now the era has come when church leaders must adapt to a new management and leadership style that embraces the best of the priestly and prophetic traditions.

Leading and managing the church is the most vital area of ministerial responsibility, particularly among African-American Churches of Christ. Many of these congregations are equipped financially to hire only a full-time minister and part-time secretary. His chief responsibility is to manage the daily affairs of the church's ministry in a particular local community. This means a careful balancing act between leadership and management. Many church leaders do not like the routine of running a well-organized ministry. They find great accomplishment and joy in the utilization of their preaching and teaching gifts. Keeping budgets in line involves the tedium of poring over statistical sheets and income projections. Expenditure requests are a monotonous and thankless job.

Leaders want to devote themselves to creative ideas, setting visionary goals, and initiating action. To accomplish their roles as effective church leaders, leaders must be good church managers of their time and schedules, both personally and organizationally. As a church administrator, a leader must define strategically what direction (vision) the church is moving toward. He must also know the specific steps (mission) to take to achieve the desired goals and objectives that will make a difference in the expansion and spiritual formation of the church.

To be able to effectively administrate the church's strategic plans of ministries, a new style of shared governance must be adopted. Church leaders can no longer afford to play politics of who will manage the church, while many competent, gifted members are mute in their voice and vote about church business. They do not seek active roles in the financial management, human resources, or other auxiliary positions. They pursue their professional careers and give token support only through their tithes and offerings. Because autocratic leadership and management styles are out of step with inclusion and consensus building, parishioners choose not to go through the hassle of service. This new role for ministers is to bring more people into the process of ownership and involvement in the life of the church. By choosing this open participatory management role, leaders will not deprive themselves of the stimulation of creative dialogue and vital information that can be exchanged for efficient and effective results. When this open-ended participatory management style is utilized, problems are solved jointly. There is a sense of ownership and stakeholders in the church's future. The role of the minister as manager allows him to reaffirm the purpose and directions of the church ministry.

Clarify Purpose and Mission

There should be no mystery about why a church exists based on the particular mission and vision that each local church has been called to in its own geographical setting. That purpose must be specific and spelled out. When this is done, only then can the church develop its own philosophy and strategy for expanding the community of faith. When the mission is clearly defined, the mission must be widely understood. In well-managed churches, both staff and congregation can articulate the church's purpose. This process is achieved through focus groups, such as Sunday School teachers, ministry directors, and church leaders.

Church leaders and lay leaders must come together to discuss and express the needs, gifts, and talents that members are willing to utilize in interfacing with the community. Lay leaders and church members are involved in this strategic process to develop goals and objectives, which demonstrates their ability to want to be responsible for making it become a reality. When this widely shared mission is understood, it begins to permeate and saturate every level of the church, and it radically transforms a community of faith.

Church leaders, who are useful in their church organizations, have developed the necessary skills to be able to successfully manage their churches to experience phenomenal growth under their leadership. The skills often associated with being good church managers are found in observing personal and family traits that demonstrate pastoral and nurturing qualities. Although these spiritual qualities are essential, they do not guarantee one's success in faithfully leading and managing a congregation. There are four essential management tools which are effective for any organization: Planning, personnel, programming, and the purse. Church leaders must make it clear to other leaders that if they are going to be held accountable for the bottom line of increasing attendance, raising contributions, equipping and releasing people for the ministry, then the leader (minister) must have the authority to implement policies and strategies.

Planning

Planning means strategizing the goals and objectives for the implementation of the church's vision. Strategic planning involves assessing the church in light of its past, present, and future. It is taking a very pro-active posture toward engagement in the issues of life that affect organizational morale and culture. Planning helps to determine what processes are important for decision-making, accountability, and the norm for congregational behavior. Planning determines the way the congregation will live together, how goals are achieved, how decisions are made, and what symbols are important and germane for organizational life. Planning facilitates the assimilation and socialization of people into the life of the church. Many African-American Churches of Christ have not developed structurally to process and assimilate new people, to track them once they have made an initial commitment of faith, and to follow them through their entire life cycle in the church for spiritual formation.

Personnel

Church leaders need to select the right personnel for ministry leadership and membership involvement. Since church organizations are primarily nonprofit corporations, the church largely depends upon a large pool of volunteers to activate and staff programs and church ministries. To maximize membership involvement, a database needs to be developed to assess spiritual gifts, talents, and interests of members which can be tapped and used to develop a specific plan of action. This can be achieved in several ways.

- Church members must emphasize—by their preaching and teaching—the priesthood of all believers.
- They must create a supportive environment that focuses on members who want to serve and find their place in the church.

- They must establish an assimilation process where people can be oriented to their obligations as members to discover and utilize their spiritual gifts.
- They must develop a comprehensive training program that moves people from membership mobilization then to ministry.

Programming

Program development is vital to the success of the church; it is the life line to serving the needs of members, as well as community involvement. Church programs should not be arbitrarily determined, but they should be devised and developed after a comprehensive needs assessment has been conducted. The needs assessment will determine what shape church ministries will take, how those ministries will be staffed, and the purpose and objectives for each ministry. The process of determining the structure for church programs is best developed through a strategic planning process. This process affords church organizations the technical skills to critically evaluate what programs are effective and what results can be measured. Church programs must be developed in light of community needs, evangelistic opportunities, assimilation of new corners, and active, as well as inactive, members.

The Purse

No organization can effectively implement its vision to make a difference without the means to raise and manage money. Church organizations are faced with the same budgetary constraints that every other organization confronts. Because of recent scandals within the evangelical community, church organizations have come under intense scrutiny to manage the church's resources and to give full financial disclosures. To effectively manage the church's assets, church managers must become adept at raising large funds through stewardship programs to offset expenditures of payroll, facility development, benevolent and mission projects. Church leaders must raise men, morale, and money to successfully move the church toward accomplishing its mission.

What Have We Learned?

As the church moves rapidly into the 21st century to meet the challenges of a post-modern culture of inner-city realism, cultural sensitivity, and institutional decline, the church finds itself becoming more irrelevant to the needs of the African-American community. Church leaders must develop new skills as managers and facilitators to address very serious problems within our communities. The church no longer lives in a church culture where we expect people to come to church. We now live in an age of mission. Church leaders must become involved in community and economic development to forge alliances with other groups.

Chapter Three
Membership Resources

The church is unique from all other organizations. Its uniqueness is rooted in its mission to be a redemptive community of faith to build up the life of its members, and to engage in a task in which its own life is to be poured out for the good of others. It is called into existence to advance a cause, by the proclamation of its message, and that is the transformation of human life. The mission of the church is threefold: 1) to help each believer to worship God with service; 2) to help every Christian to make his unique contribution by serving in a meaningful place of service, being both fruitful and fulfilled; and 3) to help individual members of the church to honor and serve one another and the world through the local church. The process through which this is accomplished is driven by developing a servant profile and helping members make their unique contribution. The purpose of this chapter is to assess several key areas that are vital to the development of church members. These key areas are the church's mission, the role of human resource planning, program development, and the process for membership development.

Understanding the Church's Mission

There should be no mystery about why the church exists. That purpose must be specific and spelled out. When this is done, only then can the church develop its own philosophy and strategy for expanding the community of faith. When the mission is clearly defined, the mission must be widely understood. In well-managed churches, both staff and congregation can articulate its purpose. When this widely shared mission is understood, it will radically transform a community of faith to transform society.

The Role of Human Resources Planning

Most churches organizationally have no existing plan to process and assimilate people, to track them once they have made the initial commitment of faith, and to follow them through their entire life cycle within the church for the purpose of spiritual formation. Current organization structures do not permit leaders to look at every constituent within the life of the church whose needs have largely been ignored. The need to develop a membership database would allow the church to take an inventory of the human resources within a local congregation, to assess spiritual gifts, talents, and interest of members. This assessment can be achieved in several ways:

- Church leaders must emphasize the priesthood of all believers.
- Leaders must create a supportive environment that focuses on members who want to serve and find their special place of service in the church.
- Leaders must establish an assimilation process where people can be oriented to their obligations as members and to discover and utilize their gifts, talents, and passion
- Leaders must develop a comprehensive training program that moves people from membership into a ministry.

Human resource planning seeks to maximize and coordinate resources of the church for the effective implementation of the church's vision. Planning affords church leaders the greatest investment and return on its resources: people, time, facilities, and money. Planning takes a very pro-active posture toward engagement in the issues of life that affect organizational morale and culture. Effective planning helps to determine what processes are important for decision-making, accountability, and what the norms will be for congregational behavior. Human resource planning shapes the way the congregation will live together, how things are done, how decisions are made, and what symbols are important and germane for organization life.

With increasing demands being made upon church organizations, competition for members with other churches, dwindling financial resources, apathy and distrust of institutional authority, church leaders will be forced to effectively implement a strategic plan for their ministry. A plan that is comprehensive in scope will address both the institutional and political needs of the church. Church organizations are legally recognized as nonprofit corporations. In many instances, they have the largest volunteer base of active supporters of any other nonprofit organizations. All too often, only about 20 percent of the members in any congregation are really involved in some capacity or giving some available or sacrificial time to the church's ministry objectives. Church leaders must realize that as people grow, so does the ministry of the church. The church must never get in the business of using people rather than developing people. In the planning process, the church will have to think developmentally about its members, and how to best meet their needs in equipping them for service (Ephesians 4:11).

In order for a church to effectively manage human resources it must take into consideration five major factors: 1) community, 2) mission, 3) organization, 4) leadership, and 5) process of a ministry. These factors constitute an effective ministry system that will bring about the maximum utilization of the church's resources. Church leaders must come to realize that congregations are not isolated from society at large, but that every community is affected at least by four primary social institutions on a continuous basis: government, education, family, and religion. The church must always keep its mission clear or it will drift aimlessly. The church exists because people who share a common religious heritage or affiliation have a desire to work out their religious faith and to offer their ministry to the community.

Program development is vital to the success of the church, and it is the life line to serving the needs of members, as well as community involvement. Church programs should not be arbitrarily determined, but should be devised and developed after some comprehensive needs assessment has been conducted. The needs assessment will determine what shape church ministries will take, how those ministries will be staffed, and the purpose and objectives for each ministry. The planning process also affords church organizations the technical skills to critically evaluate what programs are effective and what results can be measured. To be able to effectively measure the objectives of church ministries will help leaders to determine whether they have accomplished their desire purpose.

Church leaders must realize that there is a biblical mandate in the Scriptures that we must serve one another (Galatians 5:130 with our spiritual gifts (I Peter 4:10) in the right spirit (I Corinthians 13:1-3) as an expression of obedience and worship (Romans 12:1) The foundation stone is the command: through love, serve one another. The strategy for membership development is to implement a program that encompasses three phases: teaching, consultation, and service. Each phase is critical if membership development is to fulfill its intended purpose.

Phase 1: Teaching

The first step for those seeking to serve involves participation in a New Member Orientation class. This class usually lasts about six to eight hours or can be spread over a six- to eight-week period. It is a class designed to provide a step-by-step process whereby members explore who God has made them to be by identifying their passions, spiritual gifts, and temperaments. Various topics examined include goals and purposes, servanthood versus servility, biblical teaching, gift characteristics, a servant profile, ministries (service opportunities), and the responsibilities of being a servant. A variety of personal assessments are provided to assist in the identification of a person's passions, gifts, and temperaments, such as the Myers-Briggs test (personality test).

Phase 2: Consultation

Upon completion of the teaching phase, those who wish to find a place to serve make an appointment with the coordinator or ministry director. Prior to the consultation, the member is asked to review a ministry's description booklet or sheet and list three to five areas of a ministry that might be of interest to him. This list, with the servant profile, is brought to the consultation and discussed with the ministry director. The consultation is approximately an hour and designed to help the member explore specific positions within the ministries that he has identified as potential areas of service. This phase is crucial if a member is going to serve where he will be fruitful and fulfilled. At the end of the consultation, three specific areas of a ministry are identified and prioritized according to a person's passion. After the consultation, the ministry director notifies the department leaders who will be contacted by the volunteer. It is the volunteer's responsibility, however, to contact those leaders and discuss their participation.

Phase 3: Service

Once the volunteer member has completed his consultation and has discussed in detail the service opportunities identified with the appropriate ministry leader, he is ready to make a commitment. He is placed into a position according to his spiritual gifts and temperament.

Program

The development of a Ministry Resource Center is to move passive membership into an effective and coordinated system taking into consideration several key building blocks that will help everyone see the process and the outcome objective more clearly.

- Establish motivation to serve—individuals are prompted by the Holy Spirit through teaching or relationships to find a place of service within the church.
- Register prospective members for orientation to provide information and to answer questions about the church's mission and vision.
- Encourage members to attend orientation which will consist of eight hours of training (four two-hour sessions).

- Require a period of consultation. After completing the orientation, each member receives confirmation and affirmation of his servant profile and ministry possibilities through the ministry director and staff.
- Make ministry contacts. After the membership orientation, each member is responsible for exploring serving options with those ministry leaders who represent the ministries they were referred to by the ministry director and staff.
- Make a commitment to serve. Every member is a servant, and he should prayerfully discern and affirm God's lead and identify with a ministry.
- Serve the church. Once the commitment to serve with a specific ministry has been made, assimilation through orientation, training, and team identification take place. This prepares each member to begin to make his unique contribution through service.

Personnel

Select the right personnel for ministry leadership and membership involvement. Since church organizations are primarily nonprofit corporations, the church largely depends upon a large pool of volunteers to activate its program and church ministries, and the church should provide the necessary training.

The Need for Training

As our churches continue to struggle with enormous issues that people live with, the demands for in-service training will increase in our congregations. Church leaders must be able to track the emergence of new lay leaders and their development and developmental needs throughout their time with the congregation, whether it is short range or long range. The church's organizational value lies in seeing members as its most important resource. Proactively developing those people over a lifetime will be the turnaround solution for many of our churches that are in decline. As the church thinks about the needs of its people, the church should consider the following questions: Do we, as a congregation, think developmentally? Do we have a budget for developing our people? Does our church sponsor in-service training—formal or informal training? In order for this process to be more meaningful, church leaders must themselves also think developmentally about their own life, study their own management and leadership profile, and determine whether to implement a training program throughout the church.

The process of training should include the following areas:

- consider the position of the church and its direction
- align the training with the church's vision, mission, and ministry objectives
- make certain that the training supports the church's objectives
- address the training forces which guide the church and reflect its vision
- make the training consistent with the existing church's organizational system
- adhere the training to the best practices and tools for the ministry
- train as other successful churches are doing

- examine the training leadership and management competencies
- make sure that the training responds to ministry performance

These are crucial questions that church leaders must answer in developing comprehensive training programs that will mobilize members into action. Once members are recruited as personnel in the church ministry system, some principles should be clearly articulated that will serve as guidelines or policy for keeping an active pool of volunteers mobilized.

Recruitment Principles

Churches on an annual basis lose nearly 20 percent of their membership through relocation and another 10 percent because of death. Thus the average congregation needs at last 30 percent new personnel each year. The first of four principles for effective recruitment must be a constant flow of new personnel. The second principle is to make sure the person doing an effective ministry is not overloaded. The third principle is to state the importance of the ministry position of service. Encouraging people to serve by a weak challenge doesn't require very much effort. This will make the person feel that the work is not important. The result will be ineffective service with low motivation. The fourth principle is to provide a clear ministry job description of what the position requires in terms of knowledge, skills, experience, and salary. These four factors will decrease a ministry turnover and improve congregational morale.

Promotional Strategy

In order to promote and increase membership involvement, church leaders must proactively promote all the ministries of the church on a systematic quarterly basis through the church bulletins, church newsletters, testimonies, church dinners, fellowships, small group ministries, Christian education, and preaching.

Every quarter, initiate a Time and Talent Campaign. The campaign should be a concentrated effort by the director and the Ministry Life Committee to bring about exposure to the congregation as a whole. The needs should be exhibited in congregations through visual displays placed strategically throughout the church for every member to see. Brochures should be mailed three weeks in advance to ask members to check off on the appropriate card their interest in working in a specific area of a ministry or to create a new ministry. A series of special messages should be prepared by the senior minister that expose the congregation to biblical teaching in regard to the use of natural and spiritual gifts in the local church. Emphasize in each of the messages to make a commitment for the upcoming quarter. When the special messages are completed, the Ministry Life Committee should write letters and call members who completed cards to thank them for their participation and cooperation.

Two weeks after the campaign the committee should meet with various members who have expressed interest in the ministries they have selected, and conduct the process of membership development through teaching, consultation, and service. What church leaders have realized as a result of this process is that managing membership resources is vital to congregational health and morale. A definite plan of action must be developed that includes getting a commitment from members to serve, providing an opportunity for service equipping church members who feel positive about what the church is doing not only in their lives, but also in the community.

It is often assumed that good attentions alone will suffice, and that religious people and institutions are not accountable because they are insulated by the formidable wall between church and state imposed by the U.S. Constitution. Churches and religious leaders can no longer afford to be uninformed regarding their legal, nonprofit status according to the state in which they live, and the Internal Revenue code that regulates 50 1(C) nonprofit corporations.

The time has come for church leaders to become pro-active in the development of church policy that will govern how the church will respond in a given set of circumstances. The objective of this chapter is to look at the cultural, political, and institutional factors at work in the church that give rise to the need for the formation of church policy and how policy development can enhance and protect the church as a divine institution.

Chapter Four

Church Policy

With the changing nature of society, the suspicion of institutional authority, and living in a post-modern culture, the church finds itself struggling with the issue of credibility.

Cultural and Political Factors

As a result, religious scandals have shaken the evangelical community to its very foundation and have brought the church under intense scrutiny. Ministers and church leaders, due to the absence of ministerial ethics, have liability insurance to protect them from litigation. The courts are no longer exercising judicial restraint with regard to matters of religion as they did before the 1960s—a period preceding the rebellion against institutional authority.

The stature of charitable immunity once protected churches and other charitable organizations from liability for their negligent acts. In most states, it was designed to protect churches or religious organizations from exposure to financial liability. It was a stature grounded on four key premises:

- The trust fund premise that funds a religious organization was thought to be held in trust for the benefit and purposes of the charity. If the court permitted a person harmed by the church to sue the church, the money donated to the church for charitable purposes would be money diverted for unintended purposes.
- Religious employers should not be held responsible for the torts of their employees because religious employers receive no economic benefit from their employees. Thus, it would be unfair to make them financially responsible.
- Charities that perform services similar to those provided by the government should enjoy an immunity analogous to sovereign immunity.
- Immunity promotes and encourages donors to give freely to charities that

> serve society. Without immunity, the church's ability to provide the ministry would be undermined because churches are legal entities than can sue and are subject to control by state law.

The courts legally have come to recognize church actions, only if the church has taken its policies and procedures seriously. Identifying, clarifying, formalizing, documenting, adherence to, and, when necessary, amending church policies are very important measures in the eyes of the court. Most church suits involve a fight for leadership and focus on the question of who has the rightful supervision of the church's property when the church splits. Church policy becomes particularly important during such church schisms and property disputes. As a result of a cultural shift to postmodernism, churches today still enjoy a significant amount of autonomy within the wide parameter imposed by civil law.

Many church leaders and members feel that politics is an evil word, and they will contend that political action does not belong in the church. But this is a result of the inability to understand what politics is all about and what it seeks to accomplish. Political consideration governs the decision-making processes of the institutional expression of the church, just as it does in the operations of government, corporations, education, and other social institutions. It is inevitable that many of the decisions made within the institutional framework of the church will be political decisions. If one accepts the proper definition of politics and does not confuse it with partisanship, then politics does exist.

Political decisions involve three elements: coordinated allocations of scarce resources, the use of governmental machinery, and choices between public and private purposes. This can easily be translated into the framework of the church. In the church, a political decision is one which involves the allocation of scarce resources, ministerial manpower, lay leadership, church receipts, benevolence funds, and so forth. The church machinery includes church trustees, church boards, church leaders—elders and deacons. These leaders must make decisions, such as hiring more staff or putting up a new educational facility.

Church leaders who understand the political nature of scarce resources will be better equipped to participate more effectively in developing policies that recognize the political pressures that are influencing the decision-making process. Even the most superficial examination of the decision-making processes in the church supports the contention that politics is a reality of contemporary church life. As a result of political processes at work in the church, one can see evidence of patronage. "Patronage" is a political term that suggests that the distribution of resources, such as jobs or money, is based on "taking care of our own" rather than on making impartial and objective decisions on the basis of needs or competence.

The development of policy guidelines will protect the church from this kind of behavior or the abuse of church resources when a few people control the distribution of church resources. When this kind of abuse happens, it weakens the integrity of the church not only in the lives of members, but also the community at large. Politics is a vital part of church life, but patronage should never be tolerated. It creates the atmosphere of nepotism which is counter to the nature for why the church exists.

The Biblical Case for Policy Formation

Churches, as with any other business or organization, must have fundamental rules, guidelines, procedures, and customs that indicate their modus operandi as religious institutions. The church acts officially through its corporate leaders (spiritual leaders, ministers, elders, deacons, board of trustees) who legislate church policy, whether it is verbal or written. Some of the most common policy statements encountered in the church are those regarding the use of facilities, weddings, compensations, personnel issues, and bills that may be paid by the treasurer without receiving approval of the leaders or the governing board.

In Churches of Christ, there has been strong resistance in our religious history against the development of policy guidelines in our attempt to be the church of the New Testament. Churches of Christ would have no hierarchical structure, but each congregation would be autonomous and govern its own affairs following the examples of the early church. Churches of Christ believe that the church has no creed but the Bible and no authority but the Bible. One can understand and appreciate this perspective to allow the

Scriptures to govern and shape the life of the church. Policy development expressed in written form about what the church believes, practices, and how the church will govern itself does not in any way circumvent the primacy of the Bible in the life of the church. Churches need to adopt policies that clearly express the biblical interpretation of the nature and role of the church, the process of membership, church ordinances, financial support, ministry involvement, and core values. Rules that govern conduct will facilitate the church in handling and resolving church conflict much easier.

Three biblical case studies demonstrate the need for policy. The first case study is found in Exodus 18 when Moses's father-in-law, Jethro, argued the point successfully to Moses that a management system needed to be developed for the resolution of problems and conflict, and also what the policy would be in handling minor and major conflicts. Problem-solving in this case was to be decentralized to the lowest level of authority within the nation and the more serious and critical problems brought to Moses. The point of this case study is that policies were adopted to handle conflict within the entire nation of Israel.

The second case study concerns the conference or council that occurred in Acts 15, better known as the Jerusalem Conference. What is evident about this case study is that in the absence of clear teaching from Jesus, the Apostles and church leaders convened in Jerusalem to resolve a potential racial problem of how the Gentiles would be treated now that the gospel had been preached to them. The men at this conference legislated certain policies on what the church's official position would be, and this would become the watershed even to handle racial bigotry in the church.

The third case study is recorded in Acts 6 concerning the Hellenistic Widows who believed they had been neglected in the daily administration. Because of this problem, the Apostles delegated the responsibility to the people as to how to handle this problem, and they selected men who had certain qualities to respond to this problem.

When the church adopts policy guidelines, such as the case studies mentioned, it provides a plan of action or frame of reference as to how decisions will be made in a certain set of circumstances. There is no easier or better way to facilitate the implementation process in the church than by the adoption of a set of policy guidelines. There is no simpler method of avoiding unnecessary discussion of minute issues and consuming valuable time that could be devoted for more important questions than through the use of policies.

The larger a church becomes the more complicated the organizational response to its problems will be. It is critical to have already in place a series of carefully formulated policy guidelines. The central and permanent reasons for adopting policy statements are: 1) they serve as a guide for the actions and behavior of people within the church; and 2) they enable persons outside the church to anticipate how the church will respond in a given set of circumstances. The response will be one from the perspective of the entire church rather than as a single individual response. Churches of Christ—because of our emphasis on autonomy—have a tendency to fly by the seat of their pants in making decisions. Policies are guideline statements devised to assist church officials in the implementation of God's will for that specific congregation.

Church Governance

One of the central and heated arguments among African-American Churches of Christ leaders is the issue of who governs the church, the minister or the elders. This is a volatile issue that can be observed in the absence of ordained elders among African-American Churches of Christ. It is an issue of power and control. But if a church is incorporated, then legally the board of trustees controls the church's fiscal and financial assets, whereas elders and the minister would be responsible for the spiritual welfare of the members. Often this dichotomy has created a church split leaving the spiritual leaders without any legal authority unless it is clearly spelled out in the church's articles of incorporation—that trustees' power extends only to real estate with accountability to the governing church board and senior minister.

The key to church organizational accountability is an independent, informed, and involved board of directors who can also serve as spiritual leaders or shepherds. Church boards are ultimately responsible for exercising all organizational powers and managing the church's legal and spiritual affairs. They are to govern and make prudent policy decisions, oversee church operations, and hold ministry staff accountable for their actions. Examples of the kind of policies and duties of the church board would be corporate qualifications, state licensing, government funding, exempt organization classification, dissolutions, mergers, bankruptcy, lawsuits, the discipline of personnel, capital improvements, and fundraising. Once the church boards decide on a policy, it is the responsibility of the ministry staff to implement that policy.

Policy Regarding Ministerial Ordination

In Churches of Christ, the pursuits to be nonsectarian have caused church leaders to reject any formalized training to assess, evaluate, and train potential leaders for the church. Church leaders must establish criteria and standards for ministerial service in Churches of Christ. The church currently has leaders who are promiscuous and unrestrained with prudence and guidance, run the landscape of the brotherhood, creating problems and scandals. Those who are reputed to be pillars of the church refused to rescind membership within the fraternity of preachers, while their activities bring disgrace to the ministry and bring the priesthood under a cloud of shame.

No criteria or standards exists for entrance into the ministry. Anyone without ordination, confirmation, or training can become a leader. It is indicative of the current crisis that the church faces due to the lack of ministry standards for all church leaders. These standards should take into consideration the maturity traits recorded in I Timothy 3:1-7, Titus 1:5-9: the ministry traits of leading, teaching, shepherding, overseeing. As these traits become evident, leaders are able to assess the development of one's heart for God, one's heart for people, one who is a learned, one who has a cooperative spirit, and the discernment to make decisions based upon biblical principles that should be the criteria for judging a candidate for ministry.

Policy for Church Membership and Discipline

Membership allows a person to formalize his commitment to the church and to have a sense of ownership in its direction and accountability to both give and receive. Membership is actually a mutual commitment in which the church and its members help each other develop. In a policy regarding membership there should be clear expectations of what is required once a person becomes a member in relation to qualifications, reception of members, and termination of membership.

Qualifications for Membership

Any person desiring to unite with the church must attend a new member's orientation class to receive instruction dealing with biblical foundations and the church's philosophy and vision for ministry in that particular community. Each prospective member will be determined by his confession of faith expressed in baptism for the remission of sins, and transferal membership from existing congregations of the Churches of Christ. Prospective members will be informed and encouraged to participate in the life of that congregation. The suggested beginning age for membership is 12 years to adulthood.

Reception of Members

Upon approval of the prospective members' qualifications, they will be received into the membership of the church and introduced to the congregation in the next corporate worship experience. Upon satisfactory completion of this process, the individual will be publicly received back into fellowship with the church.

Policy Regarding Financial Accountability

No organization can effectively implement its vision to make a difference without the means to raise and manage money. Church organizations are faced with the same budgetary constraints that every other organization is faced with. Because of recent scandals within the evangelical community, church organizations have come under intense scrutiny to manage the church's resources and to give full financial disclosures. To effectively manage the church's assets, church leaders must become adept at raising large funds through stewardship programs to offset expenditures of payroll, facility development, and benevolent and mission projects. In these ever-increasing times and demands upon church resources, leaders must legally, morally, and ethically manage these resources. Policies should regard how money is collected and disbursed, appropriate use of signatures, development of yearly church budgets, and financial disclosures on a quarterly or yearly basis. These policies are good for congregational morale, protection of the church from audits by the Internal Revenue Service, and the forfeiture of the church's nonprofit status in addition to the seizure of church assets. This issue, probably more than any other, has hurt the church because of televangelists who were using donated funds allegedly for ministry purposes but instead were using for personal gain.

The church as an organization, as well as other institutions, is undergoing rapid change. Society has become increasingly anti-institution and anti-authority. The church must develop policies that facilitate the church's ministry in a highly volatile and complex world. The creation of policies is vital. No church can exist effectively without structure to guide congregational life. Policies must also express the values and commitments of the congregation as a whole. When policies are in tune with the values of the people, it will enable members to achieve the church's goals that are important to their spiritual growth and development. Leaders must keep in mind that the development of church policy must provide guidance for how the church will function in a given set of circumstances. These circumstances are based upon the scarcity of resources, and they protect the church from any future conflicts over the scarcity of resources in any civil litigation that might occur.

Chapter Five
Spiritual Formation

The focus of this chapter is the use of a self-directed learning theory in reducing the barriers of participation in adult religious education classes. Teaching is at the very heart of the church's mission—the transmission of spiritual values. It is in the interest of leaders to examine in the context of general voluntary adult religious education what factors are contributing to the persistent dropout of adult members. Leaders must be concerned about the lack of participation and must examine the factors which are important to adult members for participation, that is, social contact, cognitive interest, and community services as several key interests to adult learners.

The church has a two-fold purpose: to evangelize and to bring people to maturity in their faith. Adult religious education is primarily a response to faith, and it is a forum in which faith seeks to find understanding. It is through adult religious education that members are assimilated into the life of the church. If the church refuses to be concerned about the barriers to participation and to use ineffective methods of communicating and teaching, the church has failed in its task to make the Bible relevant and practical.

In recent years, African-American churches have begun to address the serious social ills that affect many African-American communities. Many leaders realize that to simply teach and educate about the spiritual needs of their members is to be derelict in their responsibility to educating the whole man. It was to this concern that Carter G. Woodson, considered the "father of Negro history," wrote in 1933 in his seminal work, *The Mis-Education of the Negro*: "Education that imparts information was not enough . . . and adequate education resulted in an output that made black people think and do for themselves, and since the black church is the only institution in the black community that is freely controlled by blacks, its main purpose should be to educate." Adult church leaders must realize the importance of understanding not only the spiritual needs of its members but also the unique psychological, emotional, and physical needs of its adult population. In this chapter, I will address: 1) the importance of adult education; 2) current assumptions about learning; 3) barriers to participation in the teaching ministry of the church; 4) the use of the self-directed learning theory and its implication for adult religious education; and 5) summary and recommendations.

The Importance of Adult Education

Adult religious education is important for reasons arising from the nature, qualities, and responsibilities of an individual person. Among these individual reasons are the following issues: the nature of the person, the stages of adult development, the nature of faith, fulfilling one's role in life, and the nature of the world. It is to these issues that the Bible was written for adults, to answer adult questions, to deal with adult problems. Adult religious education is so vital to the church because it is an opportunity to open the Bible, the textbook of the church, and to integrate biblical principles with other disciplines to foster human growth and development.

Adult education is also important because it serves several important functions. First, adult education theory encourages strong participation of the learning clientele in program planning. The major focus of Christian education should be the liberation of the human person, the development of mature decision-making abilities, the integration of knowledge and action, and a participation mode of community involvement. When church educators emphasize to members that learning is a lifelong experience and that the continuing development of adults is situated at the core of the church's educational mission, then a climate is created to foster participation in adult religious classes.

Second, adult education theory challenges church leaders to determine the purpose and curriculum of existing adult religious classes in their own congregational setting.

Third, adult education theory helps to facilitate the development of an adult membership profile to understand the nature of learners and the appropriate content that must occur in the teaching-learning context. In order for this to be done effectively, church leaders must have the professional knowledge that is needed to blend theoretical knowledge from both fields of adult education and religious education.

Current Assumption about Learning

The current assumption about learning is that there is no need to determine systematically what adult members perceive to be their educational needs or interest. Ministers and church leaders already know what adult members need and what their wants should be. This kind of assumption cannot continue if the church is going to have a vital educational ministry. It is important that church leaders understand their assumption regarding learning for it is very important to deal with adults as adults in a manner that is appropriate to their needs and style of learning.

When this is evident, church leaders can begin to think developmentally about their members. To think developmentally means that church leaders understand adult development and diverse learning theories and their use in the teaching ministry of the church. When church leaders can encourage adult members to accept responsibility for their own learning and the love of learning and interest, then the participation will increase.

Barriers to Participation

It is clear that in recent years the lack of involvement and participation in members attending Sunday school classes and midweek Bible study has seen a continuous decline in enrollment and interest. Every congregation at some point is faced with the dilemma of how to increase the level of participation in its church. How to get members involved and to take ownership of the church's mission? These are questions that leaders must seek to answer.

Leon McKenzie catalogs several important barriers to adult religious education in what he calls "conventional wisdom." These are the beliefs that characterize the theory and practice of existing adult religious education in the majority of churches:

- The conceptual development of adult religious education theory and practice rests entirely on theology or theological sciences. This means that the Bible and religious periodicals or the church are the source materials for the development of an adult religious educational theory.

- Adult religious education must be exclusively concerned with subject matters that are biblical, theological, or ecclesiastical.
- Chruch leaders should not concern themselves with human development, viewed as a whole but only those aspects of human development that are explicitly religious.
- Knowledge taken by adults on authority is education. Religious education is a process whereby adults are formed according to a given paradigm determined by church leads and are informed as to what they must believe and do.
- Religious knowledge is more important than religious learning. The transmission of ideas is at the core of adult religious education, which is primarily an intellectual endeavor.

Self-directed Learning Theory and Its Use

Most churches approach adult members from a pedagogical approach rather than from an andragogical approach. The difference in the two approaches is radically different, according to Malcolm Knowles (1980), who is a major pioneer in the field of adult education. Knowles has described several basic assumptions regarding the differences between andragogy and pedagogy learning.

Pedagogy is characterized as being teacher-directed learning, which is the foundation of education for children. Andragogy, which is the foundation for adult learning, is self-directed learning, is based upon the following assumptions:

- The concept of the learner: In teaching direct learning, the learner is seen as a dependent personality who must be directed by others in making decisions and fulfilling needs. In self-directed learning, the learner is seen increasingly as a self-directed personality who can make decisions on his own and determine his own needs.
- Experience: In teacher-directed learning, the experience of the learner is

viewed as limited or as something to build on rather than as a resource for learning. In self-directed learning, the experience of the learner is viewed as a rich resource for learning, which can be shared as part of the learning experience.

- Readiness to learn: With teacher-directed learning, the learning usually varies with physical maturity and mental development of the learner. This readiness for learning usually develops out of one's specific problems or tasks in life.
- Orientations to learning: In teacher-directed learning, the orientation to learning is usually toward specific subjects which are presented in a logical development. In self-directed learning, the orientation to learning is usually toward specific problems one faces or tasks one has to accomplish.
- Motivation: With teacher-directed learning, motivation is usually developed through external rewards or punishments (often associated with grades or promotions). But with self-

> directed learning, motivation usually involves immediate application of what has been learned.

The Bible itself proclaims that learning occurs in four areas of a person's life, as can be clearly seen in the life of Jesus. In Luke 2:52, Luke tells us that Jesus "grew in wisdom and stature and favor with God and man." It is important that leaders understand that members develop holistically. Erikson, in his book, *Adult Education*, identifies eight stages which a person will experience as he grows toward maturity: 1) Trust versus Mistrust; 2) Autonomy versus Shame and Doubt; 3) Initiative versus Guilt; 4) Industry versus Inferiority; 5) Identity versus Role Confusion; 6) Intimacy versus Isolation; 7) Generative versus Stagnation; and 8) Integrity versus Despair. These stages give great insight into human growth and development.

Abraham Maslowe, in his hierarchy of need, further enhances the various stages that adults might experience. He demonstrates that adults may be on several different levels on the strata of needs, which lead to self-actualization. Adult religious education should look to develop and provide adult members with activities that will enable them to gain insight into their spiritual needs, to examine previously formed attitudes and theories, and to see others practicing a life of faith.

The concept of self-directed learning has captured the interest of many educators in industry and education. Self-directed learning is viewed as the essence of what adult learning is all about. There are four fundamental principles at the heart of the self-directed learning theory:

- Self-directed learning initiates the process of learning that stresses the ability of individuals to plan and manage their own learning, their self-autonomy.
- Self-directed learning focuses on the individual and his own self-development, and learners are also expected to assume primary responsibility for their own learning.
- The process of learning is centered on the learner's needs.
- The role of the leader in the learning process is to act as a facilitator or guide, as opposed to content

> experts. The behaviorist in the use of self-directed learning would stress the importance of the development of learning contacts and specific learning objectives.

A self-directed learning approach to adult education has also gained a great deal of attention from Christian educators in recent years. In view of changes and development occurring in society and those anticipated in the future, it will be necessary for members to be equipped. Self-directed learning has proven thus far to be a very efficient way of increasing one's knowledge in business and education. This chapter also proposes that the self-directed learning method could be one of the important future modes of teaching in a local church.

Since the study of the Bible is the primary form of adult education in the church, leaders in their planning should ask themselves several questions as to how they can increase participation of church members in attending educational classes which are self-directed in nature:

- What are the motives for adults to participate in adult religious classes?

- Is there a relationship between the identified motives for participation in adult education programs and identified variables of age, sex, marital status, educational level, and previous participation in adult classes?
- What issues currently are members facing in their daily lives?
- Have there been major transitions that members have undergone?
- How might the church help members through these transitional times to cope and grow?

When leaders can address these questions in a substantive approach, then leaders can begin to explore how adult members learn.

The implementation of a self-directed learning program in a congregational setting must be one that is well thought out, is comprehensive, and also one that addresses the needs of the adult learner in that particular congregation. It must be a program that clearly defines the objectives that are based on congregational needs which should be conducted through interviews and surveys. After a careful needs assessment, a program should be designed that is highly visible through promotion on days and events that emphasize religious education, such as membership orientation classes and new convert classes. Classes could be structured around the following categories: 1) family relations, 2) personal development, 3) resource management, 4) life planning, and 5) spiritual growth.

When adult needs are categorized, then leaders with the joint participation of adult members can plan and develop a curriculum or classes that would focus on career planning, financial resources, family life, health and parenting, to name just a few. These kinds of classes will generate interest among members, both single, married, and divorced. These classes could be taught not only by the professional leaders, but by lay members who may be skilled in a specific area. The ultimate objective of these classes is to lead members to self-actualization, skill analysis, time management, and spiritual growth.

Church leaders will have no problem in creating ownership and responsibility for these adult classes because they are designed to be based on the needs of adult learners. Also, ask the adult learner to make a learning commitment or contract, which involves the learner to define his objectives for taking the class. For example, a class could be offered on a Christian and finances.

The adult learner is told that the class can be taken on three levels:

- The adult learner can come and receive whatever is presented, as long as he is willing to enter the discussion.
- As the adult learner takes the classes, he is encouraged to read a particular book on a Christian and finances.
- The adult learner is challenged to bring his checkbook, ledger, income tax statement, a copy of all expenditures or debts. The instructor will help the adult learner to put together a budget and help the student gain better control of his finances.

The instructor has a better sense of the overall character of the class and can better structure the curriculum to meet their needs.

The success of any self-directed learning program for adults in a congregational setting must give the adult learner:

- Choices of classes based upon his needs and levels of interest to develop the necessary skills.
- Adult religious education classes must be promoted and marketed in catalogs, church bulletins, newsletters, newspaper articles, radio announcements, and word of mouth by friends and co-workers.
- Leaders must seek to address real life issues within society that affect many of their members.
- Leaders must support and help create a climate that fosters self-directed learning.

Summary

What is the goal of adult education in the congregational setting? What core competencies, skills, and knowledge should the adult learner possess once he has completed a course of study? Howard Hendrick suggests that church leaders should have clear-cut objectives for teaching, and he suggests three goals for religious education:

- To teach people how to think. If you want to change a person permanently, make sure his thinking changes and not merely his behavior. If you change his behavior, he won't understand why he has made the change. It is only superficial and usually short-lived. The task of the teacher is to stretch the human mind.
- Teach people how to learn. Create learners who will perpetuate the learning process for the rest of their lives.
- Teach people how to work. The goal is to develop people to be self-directed and disciplined, who do what they do because they choose to do it.

This truly is self-directed learning.

Other Books by Dr. Kenneth Gilmore

The Decision Is in Your Hand

The New Covenant: Your Rights and Privileges

What Is Biblical Faith?

How To Have Success With God

Bring Me The Book

The Apostle's Doctrine

Money: God's Financial Plan For Your Life

Unmasking Satanic Lies

The Authority of The Believer

Principle Centered Living

The Power of The Tongue

Prayer, The Key To Success

God's Spiritual Laws

What Kind of Man Are You

The Battle For The Mind

Tape Series by Dr. Kenneth Gilmore

New Covenant: Your Rights	2 Tapes
What Is Biblical Faith?	2 Tapes
How To Have Success With God	5 Tapes
Money: God's Financial Plan	2 Tapes
Unmasking Satanic Lies	2 Tapes
The Authority of The Believer	4 Tapes
The Power of The Tongue	3 Tapes
God's Spiritual Laws	6 Tapes
What Kind of Man Are You?	3 Tapes
Principle Centered Living	3 Tapes
The New Testament Church, Which One Is True?	2 Tapes
The Battle For The Mind	4 Tapes
Prayer	4 Tapes

Become a Covenant Truth Partner with Kenneth Gilmore Ministries!

Because of the power that comes through fellowship, commitment and partnership, we invite you to join with Dr. Kenneth Gilmore in fulfilling the vision God has given him. Dr. Gilmore has been given a mandate to teach the Word of God in simple terms so that all can understand.

It's easy to become a Covenant Truth Partner. Simply fill out the form on page 111 and mail it to:

Kenneth Gilmore Ministries
3615 SW 13th Street
Gainesville, FL 32641

Our prayer for you is that as you enter covenant with us, God's blessings and manifold riches will be unleashed in your life.

Covenant Truth Partners have sought the Lord and received His confirmation of the worth of this ministry. Therefore, Partners are more than friends, they are loyal, trusted allies in the ministry. We value all of our Covenant Truth Partners and hold them up to God in prayer, minister to them with a personal monthly letter and offer from time to time discounted products for spiritual edification and growth.

THERE IS VALUE IN COVENANT TRUTH PARTNERSHIP!

Yes. I'd like to become a Covenant Truth Partner in prayer and financial support with Kenneth Gilmore Ministries.

____
Last Name

____
First Name Middle Initial

____
Street Address Apartment No.

____
City State Zip

You can count on me for a monthly pledge of:

❑ $1,000 ❑ $500 ❑ $100

❑ $50 ❑ $25 ❑ $______

❑ One time gift of $____________

Personal Notes

www.ingramcontent.com/pod-product-compliance
Lightning Source LLC
LaVergne TN
LVHW091004080826
845145LV00003B/1116

* 9 7 8 0 9 7 2 9 2 7 5 3 6 *